★ read ★ ... ★ out ★

KT-102-832

HORSES
AND
PONIES

Written by Julie Richardson
Edited by Carol Watson
Illustrated by Libby King

CARNIVAL

The Horse and its History

There was a type of horse on earth sixty million years ago, long before man himself arrived. However, it was not until four thousand years ago that man first used the horse, and it was many years later that he began to breed horses to suit his needs.

Points of the Horse

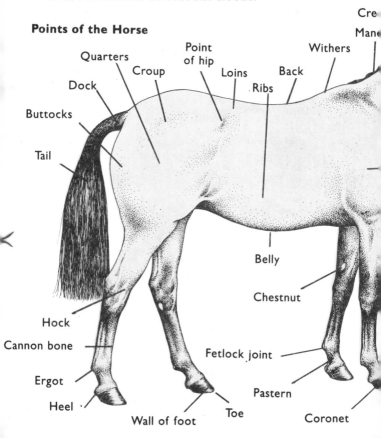

At first people ate horses; then they realised how much more useful they would be pulling carts and ploughs and carrying heavy loads. Eventually, men learned to ride horses and used them to go out hunting and into battle. Horses drew carts on farms and carriages in towns, and then they took part in sports such as jousting, racing, jumping and polo.

Today horses are still used for work and for giving pleasure to millions of riders.

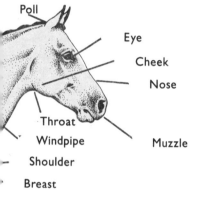

Poll

Eye

Cheek

Nose

Throat

Windpipe

Muzzle

Shoulder

Breast

nee

It is important to be able to identify all the 'points' of a horse to be able to judge a good horse or pony. The height of a horse is always measured in 'hands'.

Good or Bad Shape?

Horses, like people, are built differently and this affects the way they perform, how strong they are and how long they will be able to live an active life. The shape of the horse, or the way it is 'put together' is called *conformation*. Some people are very clever at spotting 'good' or 'bad' horses, but there are certain points that are easy to look for and to avoid.

At first glance the horse should look good and well-proportioned. Smallish heads with ears to match, and big, honest eyes are best. Broad foreheads mean intelligence, but wild eyes show a bad temper.

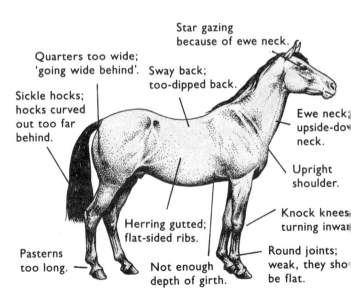

Star gazing because of ewe neck.

Quarters too wide; 'going wide behind'.

Sway back; too-dipped back.

Sickle hocks; hocks curved out too far behind.

Ewe neck; upside-down neck.

Upright shoulder.

Knock knees turning inward.

Herring gutted; flat-sided ribs.

Pasterns too long.

Not enough depth of girth.

Round joints; weak, they should be flat.

Bad Conformation

Shoulders should have a good slope, chests should be broad, backs short and girths deep.

It is very important for horses to have good legs and feet. Both pairs of feet should match in size and shape, and they should be neither too flat nor too upright.

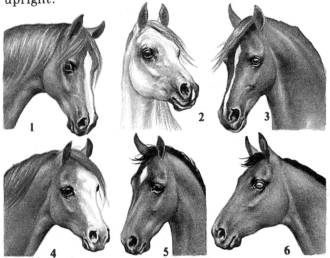

Face markings
I Blaze – white marking from the forehead down the face to the muzzle. 2 Snip – isolated white mark between the nostrils. 3 Stripe – similar to blaze, but narrower. 4 White face – white covers the forehead and nose in a broad band down to the muzzle. 5 Star – any white forehead mark. 6 Wall eye – white or blue eye, caused by lack of iris pigment.

Bad Habits

Bad habits are biting, kicking, rearing, napping (refusing to do as it is told), bucking a lot, weaving (waving the head from side to side), crib-biting and windsucking.

Colours and Markings

A horse's colour is that of its coat (body colour) and points (mane, tail, lower legs and muzzle). Its markings are the white hairs on the face and lower legs. The two most common body marks are called saddle marks – white patches under the saddle – and girth marks, which are white patches under the girth.

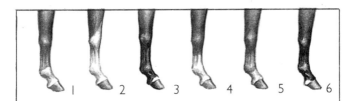

Leg markings
1 Coronet 2 Fetlock 3 Pastern 4 Heel 5 Sock
6 Stocking. White leg markings covered with black spots
of hair are called 'ermine'.

The five main colours are:
bay, black, brown, chestnut,
and grey. The horses shown
below are:

1 Grey	7 Strawberry roan
2 Liver chestnut	8 Palomino
3 Bay	9 Spotted
4 Iron Grey	10 Dun
5 Chestnut	11 Skewbald
6 Piebald	12 Black

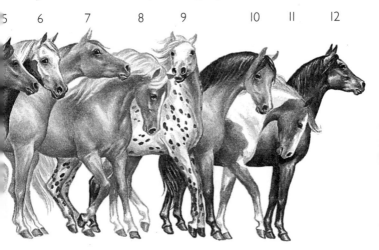

Types of Horse and Pony

Many horses and ponies are pure-bred. This means that they are registered in a book called a 'stud' book, which lists all the pedigrees of that breed for many generations. However, most riding horses and ponies are not pure-bred. They are a mixture of breeds and are known for their *type* rather than their breed.

Riding Pony

Ponies bred today are really all 'riding ponies'. Those in Britain, however, are usually a mixture of Welsh pony and other British breeds. The best of them are also part-Thoroughbred or part-Arab. They are between 13 and 14.2 hands.

Polo Pony

Polo ponies are still called ponies although they are now all over 15 hands. A long neck, good shoulders and powerful quarters makes a fine, wiry pony and a good goal scorer. Most polo ponies are Thoroughbred.

Cob

Cobs are honest little horses, famous for their strength, stamina and good temper. The best come from Ireland and Wales. The cob has a big body, rather short legs and is no higher than 15.3 hands.

Polo pony

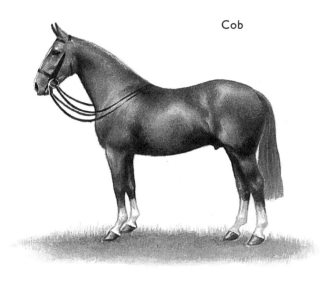

Cob

Hunter

Any horse can be ridden out hunting, but a true hunter is a certain type. It is a quality, strong animal, with a deep, short body and strong legs with good bones. The height can be between 15.3 hands to 17 hands.

A good hunter should have the courage and stamina to hunt two days a week. It should be able to stand quietly when necessary, gallop, jump safely and not pull too much. It must also ignore the hounds. To kick a hound is the worst thing a hunter can do in the eyes of the Master of the Hunt.

Hunters are usually British, and Ireland is well-known for breeding some of the best in the world.

Hunter

Hack

The hack is a light riding horse. It can be any breed, but is usually Thoroughbred, Anglo-Arab or part-bred Arab.

The name 'hack' is British, and many years ago a 'covert hack' was an elegant horse used to carry its master to the hunt meet. A 'park hack' was an even more elegant horse which society ladies and gentlemen used for riding in the park.

Hacks are never more than 15.3 hands high. Sometimes ladies ride them side-saddle in the showring.

Hack

Horses of the World

Arab

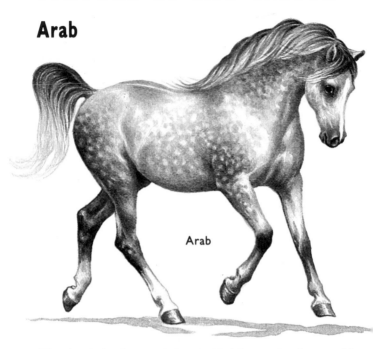

Arab

The Arab is the most beautiful horse in the world. It is also the oldest (over 4,000 years) and the purest. It has given its beauty and strength to every other breed including the Thoroughbred.

The Arab has a short, strong back, sound legs and a high, banner-like tail. These horses are usually grey, chestnut or bay. Arabs are fiery, but kind, and are used as all-round riding horses, carrying far heavier loads than their size suggests. An Arab crossed with a Thoroughbred is called an 'Anglo-Arab'.

Thoroughbred

The Thoroughbred is the fastest horse in the world. Its fine, well-proportioned body has made it famous.

This horse was first bred in England more than 250 years ago from three eastern horses crossed with British mares. Like the Arab, it has since been crossed with other breeds to pass on its good qualities.

The Thoroughbred is a light animal, with a beautiful head, elegant neck, good sloping shoulders, hard legs and strong quarters. It can be brown, bay, grey, chestnut or black and is usually between 16 and 16.2 hands.

Thoroughbred

British Ponies and Horses

The mountain and moorland ponies which first came from the British Isles can now be seen all over the world. There are nine major breeds:

Dales
These sturdy ponies are small versions of the heavy horse (see page 19). They have a lot of hair on their heels (called 'feathers'), strong, short legs, compact bodies and short necks with elegant pony heads. They are used for riding, but are also good driving ponies. Height: up to 24.2 hands. Colours: black, dark brown, grey.

New Forest
These ponies have good legs and feet, but rather plain heads. Height: up to 14.2 hands. Colours: any but piebald and skewbald.

Connemara
Attractive ponies which come from western Ireland. They are hardy, sound, intelligent and kind. They are natural jumpers and make good cross-country ponies. Height: up to 14.2 hands. Colours: grey, black, bay, brown and dun.

Dartmoor

Dartmoors are good-looking and make good riding types. They are sensible and sure-footed. Height: up to 12.2 hands. Colours: bay, brown, black.

Fell

These are a lighter version of the Dales Ponies. They are sensible and used for trekking. Height: up to 14 hands. Colours: black, dark brown, bay, grey, dun.

Exmoor

Exmoors are the purest native ponies. Their foreheads are broad, ears short and thick and nostrils wide. They have unusual hooded eyes, known as 'toad' eyes, and thick coats. They make tough riding ponies. Height: up to 12.3 hands. Colours: bay, brown, dun or grey.

Highland

These are the biggest and strongest native ponies and come from the mountains of Scotland. They have large bodies and are still used to carry shot deer down from the glens. Height: up to 14.2 hands. Colours: dun, black, bay, grey.

Shetland

These are the smallest ponies in the world. They are docile, loveable and tough. They have small heads, compact bodies, short legs and thick manes and tails. Height: up to 106.6 cms. Colours: black, brown, bay, piebald, skewbald.

Welsh

There are four types of Welsh pony. These types are called 'sections'.

Section A

These are Welsh Mountain ponies and are probably the most popular and prettiest of the native ponies. They have lovely faces, small muzzles and large, intelligent eyes. They move quickly and freely and have strong legs and hard feet.

Section B

The Welsh Pony is bigger than the Welsh Mountain pony and is known as the finest riding pony in the world. These animals make wonderful competition ponies for children. This breed is a mixture of Welsh Mountain and the Welsh Cob.

Section C

Welsh Cobs are bigger and stronger than Welsh Mountains with a fine trotting action. They are used for driving and riding and also jump well.

Section D

These too, are Welsh Cobs, but are bigger than Welsh Cobs in Section C. They are courageous and determined.

Welsh Mountain Pony (Section A)
Height: up to 12 hands.
Colours: any except broken colours.

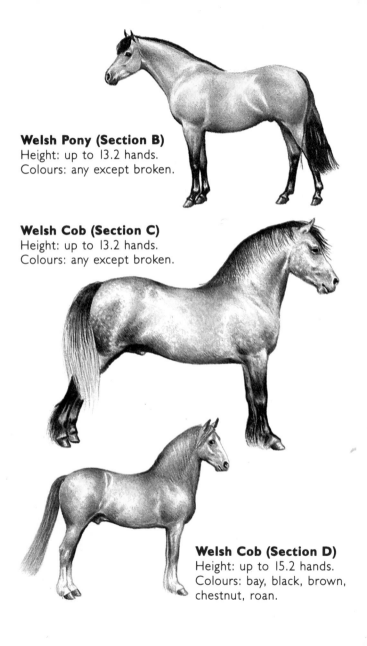

Welsh Pony (Section B)
Height: up to 13.2 hands.
Colours: any except broken.

Welsh Cob (Section C)
Height: up to 13.2 hands.
Colours: any except broken.

Welsh Cob (Section D)
Height: up to 15.2 hands.
Colours: bay, black, brown,
chestnut, roan.

Hackneys

Hackneys are mainly driving horses and you can see them all over the world in studs and in the showring. Their colours are bay, brown, black and chestnut – often with white stockings. They can be up to 16 hands high. These horses are best known for their amazing high-stepping trotting action. They lift their knees high and suspend their forelegs for a moment at each stride they take.

Hackney Ponies

These are treated as a separate breed from the horses, and are connected with the trotting ponies from Westmoreland. They look like small versions of Hackney horses, and have the same way of trotting and similar personalities. Their colouring is the same as Hackney horses and they are up to 14.2 hands in height.

The Heavies

The best-known British heavy horses are Shires, Clydesdales and Suffolk Punches.

A shire horse ready to pull a brewery dray in the show ring. Heavy horse manes and tails are plaited with coloured ribbon unlike the plaiting used for riding horses.

Shires

These are probably the biggest horses in the world. They often weigh more than a tonne and can be up to 18 hands high. Their colours are black, grey, brown and bay.

Clydesdales

These are more active than Shires with very strong feet and lower legs. Their colours are bay, black, brown and roan and they can be up to 16.2 hands high.

Suffolk Punch

These are also very active with very little 'feather' on the heels. They are chestnut in colour and can be up to 16.2 hands high.

Riding

A horse has four ways of moving forward. These are called 'gaits' or 'paces'. They are walk, trot, canter and gallop.

Walk This is made up of four steps and is called 'four-time'.

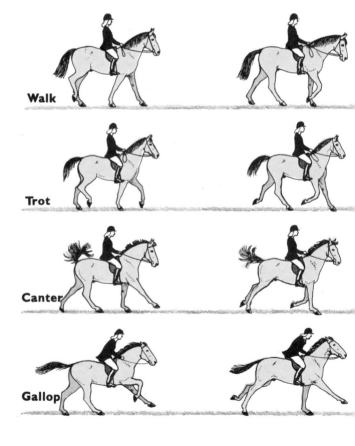

Walk

Trot

Canter

Gallop

Trot This is two-time. The near-fore leg and the off-hind leg move together, as do the off-fore and the near-hind leg.

Canter The canter is in the three-time.

Gallop This is the fastest pace. It is in four-time like the walk. Each hoofbeat can be heard separately.

Jumping

Horses are natural jumpers, but they don't jump unless they have to. If loose in a field, a horse will go round an object rather than jump over it.

The approach

As it is about to jump, the horse lowers its head, stretches its neck and looks down.

Take-off

The horse shortens its neck, gathering its hocks beneath it. Then it lifts its forelegs, bends its knees and thrusts upwards.

Suspension

While in the air, the horse gradually unfolds its knees and restretches its neck.

Landing

The horse lands on one foreleg, quickly followed by the other and then the hindlegs. Its head and neck rise to help it balance.

Tack

Tack is the name given to the complete saddle and bridle outfit worn by the horse. The bridle and bit allow the rider to change pace and direction.

The most basic bridle is called the snaffle bridle, which has only a few straps and fittings. It can be used with a single bit of any type, and can be fitted with any noseband.

Most saddles are leather and are built around a skeleton of wood or metal called a 'tree'. This holds them in shape. Saddle trees can be 'rigid', which means they don't give, or 'spring', which means they do. Both kinds break easily and if not mended will injure the horse's back.

It is important that the saddle fits the horse properly. It should not rub the horse sore and should be restuffed regularly. The seat should fit the rider properly.

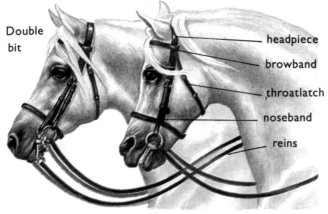

Double bit

headpiece
browband
throatlatch
noseband
reins

Snaffle bit

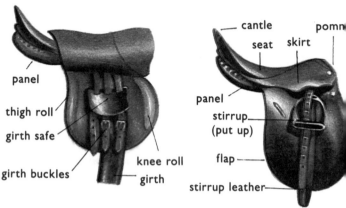

There are many types of saddle. The most common are general purpose, jumping and dressage. They all keep the rider in the best position for a particular task.

Other tack:

Halters
These are made of rope or nylon and are used for leading or tying up the horse.

Girths
are used to keep the saddle secure. There are many types, but leather and string are both good.

Stirrup leathers
these must be strong or can be dangerous.

Stirrup irons
usually about a centimetre wider than the rider's foot so that they don't trap it.

Lunge rein and whip
are useful for exercising the horse in circles without a rider on its back.

Grooming

Grooming keeps horses fit and healthy, as well as improving their appearance.

To keep a horse well groomed you need these items:

Dandy brush *Removes mud and sweat.*
Body brush *and metal curry comb. Brush removes dust and grease, comb cleans brush after every stroke.*
Rubber curry comb *Removes sweat marks and mud.*
Mane comb *Pulls (shortens) mane and tail by removing hairs.*

dandy brush

body brush

water brush

rubber curry comb

hoof pick

metal curry comb

mane comb

sponge

sweat scraper

stable rubber

Water brush *Washes feet and damps mane and tail.*
Sponges *One used for wiping eyes, ears and muzzle, another for wiping dock and sheath area.*
Hoof pick *Removes mud and stones from under the hoof.*
Stable rubber *Polishes coat.*
Sweat scraper *Removes excess water from coat.*

Clothing

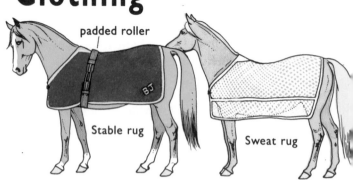

padded roller

Stable rug

Sweat rug

Most horses wear a rug at some time. There are rugs used in the stable to keep the animals warm; one is a night rug and the other is a woollen day rug. In hot weather a cotton summer sheet keeps the horse cool and free of flies. If a horse gets sweaty there is a sweat rug like a string vest, which keeps the horse warm until it dries.

A waterproof New Zealand rug is used to protect a horse at grass in cold, wet weather.

There are also boots and bandages which can be worn to guard the legs from injury. Brushing boots protect between the knee and fetlock, while over-reach boots protect the coronet and heel. Bandages offer support and warmth. Exercise bandages are used during work; stable bandages at rest.

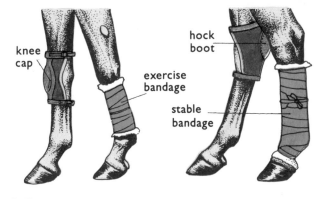

knee cap

hock boot

exercise bandage

stable bandage

Shoes

Horses nowadays have to wear shoes to stop their feet wearing away on modern roads and becoming sore. The horny outside wall of the foot grows in the same way as human nails. When horses live in the wild this is worn away naturally and does not need trimming. If a horse wears shoes this horn cannot be worn down at all; so every month a man called a farrier has to take off the shoes, 'rasp' the horn and replace or renew the shoes.

There are two types of shoeing: hot or cold. In hot shoeing the farrier moulds red-hot iron to fit the horse's hoof before nailing it on. The horse does not have any feeling in this part of its hoof, so it does not have any pain.

The basic shoe is a hunter shoe. Here are some other kinds.

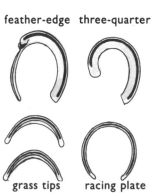

feather-edge three-quarter

grass tips racing plate

Feeding

The horse's natural food is grass which it eats slowly for most of the day. A horse can live well on grass as long as it is not working too hard and the grass is at its best. However, at other times the horse needs extra food such as oats and horse nuts, or hay.

When snow is on the ground, or the grass is very poor, hay is given to replace bulk. Hay is simply dried grass. It is best when it is between six and 18 months old, and should never be brown or mouldy.

Grazing

Horses need at least an acre of grassland each if they are to remain fit and healthy. Grazing keeps horses healthier and happier than stabling. However, if they are needed for heavy work, horses are usually stabled so that food, exercise and regular grooming are guaranteed.

Horses are bad grazers. They leave large areas of grass untouched and spoil others with their droppings. Removing the droppings helps to stop this, but the ideal thing is to allow the field to 'rest' for a few months each year by removing the horses. It is also important to check the field regularly for harmful objects which might injure the horse.

ragwort   privet   deadly
                                 nightshade   hemlock

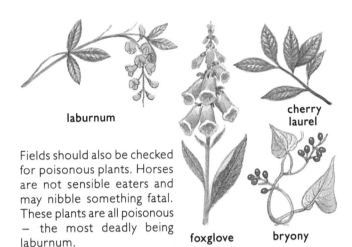

laburnum

cherry laurel

Fields should also be checked for poisonous plants. Horses are not sensible eaters and may nibble something fatal. These plants are all poisonous – the most deadly being laburnum.

foxglove

bryony

Hard Food

Horse-food other than grass and hay is called 'hard food'. Of all hard food, oats are the best grain. All grain should smell sweet and be clean and should be fed bruised, rolled or crushed. Barley can be boiled whole and maize flaked.

Bran is often added and can be mixed with other grain to add bulk and help digestion. Horse nuts are an easy-to-use pelleted mixture of balanced food.

crushed oats

whole barley

flaked maize

bran

sugar beet

nuts

Stabling

When horses are stabled they rely upon their owners because they are unable to fend for themselves. Every day they need to be mucked out, fed, watered, exercised, groomed and rugged up if the weather is cold.

A horse can be stabled in a loosebox, where it can move freely, or in a stall where it is tied up.

A loosebox should be light and airy and big enough. (The average size box is about four metres square.) It should be ventilated so that any draughts are higher than the horse's back.

Popular bedding materials are straw, peat, wood shavings and sawdust.

A loosebox bedded with straw and fitted with automatic drinker, corner manager, hay net fittng and good ventilation.